# TABLE OF CONTENTS

# FOREWORD

TWO SIDES OF WAR
Grantland Rice

"All wars are planned by older men
In council rooms apart
Who call for greater armament
And map the battle chart.

But out along the shattered field
Where golden dreams turn gray,
How very young the faces were
Where all the dead men lay.

Portly and solemn in their pride,
The elders cast their vote
For this or that or something else,
That sounds the martial note.

But where their sightless eyes stare out
Beyond life's vanished toys
I've noticed nearly all the dead
Were hardly more than boys."

Here are three narrative poems about war. In them, you may see the sightless eyes of boys from everywhere in America, who should properly be called men. And you may see the eyes of the companions who fought with them and lived for decades with the precious burden of noble and sad memories. In their minds' eyes, their hearts and their dreams.

These narratives were first written as stage presentations with speakers, music and visuals. They have been presented in a few theaters and commemorative events in California. Their focus is on the hearts and minds of the men under fire.

The  planning, strategy, tactics, logistics and training are not told in detail, but only in service to the stories of those men. The stories are presented in the order in which they were written.

We want the rhythmic, rhyming nature of the verses to bring the reader closer to the multi-dimensional emotional impact of a stage presentation or movie.  That's what the shorter poetry about wars has done.

It is what the epic and narrative poems did in primitive times.  We fervently wish this trilogy will be read and re-read, in solitude and aloud, perhaps even by small groups sharing the reading in family rooms or classrooms.

Finally, we will be blessed if the reading prompts reflection on the fact that, in the 21st century, man has not yet successfully created alternatives to war.  We inherited bloodshed, but do not have to bequeath it.

# DEDICATION

Dedicated here to my patient and helpful loved ones; Lynn and Sloane Pettit and Jessica Pettit Scarffe.

With deep gratitude to many for advice, encouragement and assistance.

Foremost among these is Toby Willaby of ATS Advertising, talented and creative problem-solver.

Thanks, also, to talented artist, John Finger (www.fingerart.com) for many fine drawings of the action and personalities in *The Battle of Bull Run.*

And my friends from drought-stricken Northern California. They are well-irrigated and insure the same condition for me. They are a fertile source of encouragement and advice. They know who they are.

## BEDFORD AMERICA

Rise at dawn in Bedford, Virginia. You may see a solitary American Eagle as he comes from the mists in the verdant, timbered slopes of the Blue Ridge mountains….. rising north and west.

The proud raptor may fly eastward, growing in your vision, even as he soars upward toward the clouds, always looking downward, honoring souls from Bedford….. heroes now at rest.

He seems to know, that on one day, those heroes bore more of America's burden than one could ever dream, becoming all of us then, transforming a hamlet…. to national hallowed ground.

He will come again on other days, evanescent and enduring as tide and memory; in grand salute to this humble place, home of true American Eagles….. to whose wings we all are bound.

June 6, 1944: D-Day. Freedom's day. America's day. Eisenhower's day. Britain's and Canada's day. Allied Expeditionary Forces day. BEDFORD'S DAY. Then, as now, just one in 50,000 Americans were from Bedford. But on that day, on those beaches, one in 100 American fatalities were from Bedford; a price beyond reason, the dearest price on the longest day.

This lovely town, nestled in the lee of the Blue Ridge mountains in Central Virginia, just 50 miles west of Appomatox Court House, redolent with memories of Robert Lee and Grant and Sherman and Pickett and savagery and honor in combat from the beginning of our nation; noble and sad memories, forming an invisible shroud around a bucolic, beautiful, peaceful and old American village.

This is a story and a song of Bedford; about the sons of Bedford and their companions on that iconic day. Who were they? How did they get there? What did they do there? What are the legacies they carried to the fight and the ones they left to us? We will plumb for meaning in this unique American story; and then each of us can define that meaning for ourselves, in our hearts.

Bedford

Playing ball and hunting game, they were poker playing schemers
And yearning then past the Blue Ridge hills, learning to be dreamers
They were treasured in that village, and were copper-penny bright
From its mills and farms, road gangs and stores, they would go to the fight.

*They were in their late teens and early twenties. None, not one, had gone past high
school; many had dropped out; they all saw their futures in local jobs or family farms;
most of them smoked and drank beer; but they were law abiding, went to church; they
seem like Norman Rockwell's boys next door.*

The simple pleasures of their days, in those years, came from sharing
In this outpost of the Frontier Code, life required caring
And caring they got in Bedford, from a trove of treasured friends
As they toughened mind and muscle to prepare for harsher ends.

*They were listening to the ominous news from Europe and they were listening
to the father figures in their lives; they must have believed that they would be going
to war like the generations before. But their focus was on their Blue Ridge lives,
close to nature and each other.*

Most were blood-tied back to Bedford, to its founders and beyond
Strong-spirited English rebels who would break King George's bond
Strength seen again at First Manassas and then at Belleau Wood
Lay coiled in wait for Normandy, to drive them as it should.

*Bedford men had been in all the wars and their cemeteries bore witness.*
*They were from the Virginians who, unstintingly, made the death charge*
*with Pickett at Gettysburg and for whom Robert E. Lee had broken with his*
*northern friends and classmates.*

At first they joined for friendship and a dollar a week in pay
On Monday nights at the armory, they learned the soldier's way
And so in the quiet '30's, they were viewed with high regard
Bedford's citizen soldiers in Virginia's National Guard.

*Being in "the guard" was as normal as going to church or playing ball; a concrete*
*preparation for what might come; approbation from their neighbors and elders; a*
*learning experience unmatched by any of their schools. It was the thing to do for*
*about 30% of the men their age in Bedford.*

As the girls watched their smart parades, sparks began to fly.
Romance was everywhere in Bedford, hearts were flying high
They courted with the chivalry expected by tradition
But left sweet, tearful lovers for their country's noble mission.

*Before they went to war, about a third of them had married and*
*another third had steady intendeds, one was a father and another a father-to-be;*
*all the girls were from Bedford County.*

As the decade turned, the world shook, Hitler was on the move
America's youth were learning they might have much to prove
In October, 1940, the expected call brought tears
The Bedford boys would mobilize and the town would face its fears.

*In the early fall of 1940, it was clear that President Roosevelt was moving the country toward a war footing. The first peacetime draft in American history was passed in September, increasing the size of the army tenfold. A state of emergency was called. An Office of Production Management was formed. War preparations were being made while being denied. All eyes were on Britain, the rest of Europe and Hitler. In October, the word came down. Company A would be activated in early 1941. They were told it would be for one year and they must have wanted to believe it.*

In February '41, the Fireman's Band would lead
As they marched with pride to a hoedown where Bedford bid Godspeed
Next day, red-eyed and sleep bereft, they were on an eastbound train
They slept, but likely could not dream of their town's impending pain.

*This was a real Blue Ridge country shivaree, it lasted all night and, in the morning, their girls and hardy friends were still with them on the train platform, with whiskey and Coca Cola in continued celebration.*

The Bedford boys were chosen as the heart of Company A
Ninety-eight of two hundred strong to train for destiny's day
Knowing not of their combat future, building teamwork and skill
Getting fit for the vanguard, to lead in the charge to the kill.

*Company A, two hundred men, part of the 1st Battalion of the 116th Regiment in the 29th Infantry Division; Bedford's own Captain Taylor Fellers commanded the Company. He had not gone beyond high school, but was a diligent officer dedicated to an army career. The Regiment and the Division were commanded by hard-nosed, spit and polish, West Pointers, Colonel Charles Canham and General Charles Gerhardt. All three officers would serve with honor at Omaha Beach.*

Three of them earned higher rank, leading Bedford's way to war
Honored charge of dear friends from home was the burden that they bore
They fulfilled that heavy commitment with dignity and pride
Through the numbing years of training for the fight in which two died.

*Captain Taylor Fellers, Platoon Commander Lieutenant Ray Nance and Company Master Sergeant John Wilkes; all sons of Bedford, were truly in America's lead at Omaha Beach; they earned special memory at home and in America. The Bedford boys were in charge of Company A.*

Queen Mary, Queen of the Ocean, first built for sea going grace
Now rigged as a Spartan troopship, soldiers squeezed in every space
Eleven-thousand swarmed aboard in September '42
The Bedford boys were on their way to destiny's rendezvous.

*For eighteen months, they had trained at Fort Meade, Maryland; bivouacked at Camp A.P. Hill, Virginia; trained again at Camp Blanding, Florida, to finally board a train headed to Camp Kilmer, New Jersey. There, they were re-equipped, loaded with the latest and best combat rigging and mustered aboard the Queen Mary. Country boys in awe of what they were experiencing and thoughts of what they might become.*

On a gray and raining October day, they reached Britain's shore
Still not knowing of their role in Eisenhower's plan for war
But pleased they were still together, in this bustling distant land
Depending more now on each other for friendship's welcome hand.

*They landed in Greenock, Scotland, in the dismal autumnal north, and entrained again, in cramped old cars of the London, Midland and Scottish Railway. Barrage balloons and blackout curtains told them they were closer to war. As they headed south, the country reminded them of Virginia; they were offered tea and crumpets. The experience was intriguing and they slept fitfully as night fell. In the morning they debarked at Salisbury Plain, southwest of London; their barracks were called Tidworth, an old British Cavalry post of steel, brick and rock, cold and austere. They were just ten miles from the ancient mysteries of Stonehenge, a fitting metaphor for their deep wonder, but theirs was a wonder tinged with trepidation.*

They admired Taylor Fellers, his wisdom and his daring
His easy, profane country style, his Bedford way of caring
He came from their ranks to take their lead, with confidence and verve
He loved them and despised their grief, but he never lost his nerve.

*He was a disciplinarian. But he had empathy. He would reduce them in rank for misbehavior, he would set a standard for physical excellence, he established trust and cared for them. He was direct and guileless in manner and speech. He told others of his concern for his men and asked special treatment for them when he could. Following their pre-invasion briefing, he told his Regimental Commander, Colonel Charles Canham, three ranks senior, "Colonel, I can take one Browning automatic rifle and get on that cliff and deny that beach to any infantry group"--- and to a group of newcomers; "My name is Captain Taylor Fellers. This company will be in the leading wave of infantry in the invasion of Europe. You men will be part of a great force to end the war. Good luck!" He was twenty-nine years old.*

They spent twenty months in England, mainly on the bloody move
They trained and drilled and trained again, till they'd nothing left to prove
Suffering stifling old stone barracks and tents that leaked and stank
In cold and fog, rain, mud and heat that respected no man's rank.

*The training was intense. It was now clear that Company A would be the aggressive first force ashore on D-Day. All were required to earn the Expert Infantryman's Badge by running one-hundred yards in twelve seconds; completing thirty-five pushups and ten chinups; clearing an obstacle course in a sprint and qualifying as marksmen with the Colt .45 pistol; the Garand M-1 and the Browning Automatic Rifles. Failure to qualify meant reassignment to non-combat status. Because of attrition, promotions and transfers, the original Company A Bedford contingent of ninety-eight was down to thirty-six. Additional qualified men were fed into the Company to keep its strength at two-hundred. The qualifiers then conducted many rehearsals of their beach-assault, in the face of live ammunition, sometimes twice a day.*

Endless now, in early June, the invasion convoys rolled
Through florid English hamlets, past admiring British souls
The quiet display of Allied will was stunning but serene
And the world sensed the surging of a massive war machine.

*This was the greatest parade ever seen in England and ever to be seen. Men from the free world, almost 160,000 of them, with trucks, tanks, jeeps, weapons of all kinds -- a rolling armada. They traversed the south of Britain, through the florid hamlets, welcoming the spirit of Godspeed as it flowed to them from thousands of war-weary families, the young and the old, many with flowing tears in loving accent to the heartfelt hope that they would see these young men again.*

Fatigue had muted hope in Britain, from four long years of trial
Of relentless daily hardship, of insult and denial
Of shivering as cold grief and fear were chilling every home
But they watched and shed warm tears that June for sons they'd never known.

*The stoic dignity and unquenchable pride of the English people were seen by all the allied warriors as they joined with Britain's own to embark on a massive and serious business, with an equally massive array of weapons, supplies and equipment, the tools of their trade. It seemed that the thanks being extended to the troops in many different, and mostly quiet, expressions, was not for the long awaited rescue that success would bring toBritain, but for the gifts of courage those troops were bringing to the world.*

Ships packed Southern England's docks, loading troops for the invasion
Hundreds of ships boarded fighting men from every Allied nation
One hundred fifty-six thousand plus for sixty miles of beach
But Company A's two-hundred would go first into the breech.

*Company A loaded at Weymouth on the HMS Empire Javelin with the rest of the 116th Regiment. It was 4 June, 1944. That afternoon, they learned the invasion had been postponed to 6 June. Most spent the waiting time gambling, sharpening knives and bayonets, trying to sleep; while their senior officers visited the chart room and pondered the coming storm. Company A would be first off the ship, two-hundred men in six landing craft called LCA's; Taylor Fellers and twenty-nine chosen men would be the first of the first.*

HMS Empire Javelin

*At 4a.m., the morning of 6 June, the Bedford boys were on deck, ready to board their LCA's, not knowing that most of them would be dead before nightfall, and listening to this message from General Eisenhower, the Supreme Allied Commander.*

*"Soldiers, sailors and airmen of the Allied Expeditionary Force. You are about to embark upon the Great Crusade, toward which we have striven these many months. The eyes of the world are upon you. The hopes and prayers of liberty-loving people everywhere go with you. In company with our brave allies and brothers-in-arms on the other fronts, you will bring about the destruction of the German war machine, the elimination of Nazi tyranny over the oppressed peoples of Europe, and security for ourselves in a free world."*

*Captain Fellers thanked his men for their hard work during training and asked them to be careful. "This is it", he added, "This is the real thing".*

Their ship lurched in black rough seas, 12 miles off Normandy's shore
At 4.a.m. the sixth of June, now rigged and ready for war
They clambered to the landing crafts that would carry Bedford's brave
To bloody, tragic destiny in America's first wave.

*They called out to each other, exchanging expletives and good wishes as they settled in the LCA's; and as they were lowered into the water for the twelve mile run to the beach. Then seasickness overcame some and anxiety struck most. They were following LCA 910 with Captain Fellers and the chosen 29. It would arrive right on time: 6:30a.m.*

Panzer guns were placed and trained to besiege the allied assault
The plans in place to bombard those guns were plans besieged by fault
So Company A was hit by crossfire, relentless and severe
Earning high historic honor with their blood, their lives, their fear.

*They had been told that massive pre-invasion bombardment would decimate the known German gun positions. The Navy's big guns were not effective for reasons still unclear. Three-hundred-twenty-nine B-24 "Liberators" had indeed dropped thirteen-thousand bombs between 5:55 and 6:14 a.m. They did not hit the beach and create sheltering craters for the infantry as promised. Because of cloud cover, the bombs were poorly aimed, landing inland, killing cows and Frenchmen. It is reported that, even with accuracy, few craters would have resulted because the bombs used were not good for that purpose. This was error, bordering on scandal.*

In the brutal heat of war, irony shows its cruel way
The strongest can be denied a chance to ever join the fray
Frank Draper, a champion athlete with a champion soldier's skill
Was chest-shot in his landing craft, the first Bedford boy killed.

*He had been a baseball star in the Army,
leading the 116th Regiment's Yankees to the championship
of the European Theater. He had been a three sport star in high
school, coming across the tracks from a poor family. His native
skills made him a strong soldier. He was described as calm,
decisive and organized; the only Bedford boy who kept a diary.
He left a fiancé in Bedford, to mourn with his hardscabble
family. He was the victim of a low probability hit by one of the
random anti-tank bullets that were sporadically
reaching the incoming LCA's.*

Taylor Fellers' landing craft stopped in an eerie pre-storm gloom
And twenty-nine men went down the ramp, in silence, to their doom
He led them thirty yards in surf to a hillock in the sand
Then they charged and there they died as the crossfire storm began.

*He thanked the British skipper of his LCA for getting them in on time. That was the
last time a D-Day survivor heard his voice. He went first down the ramp, leading his
men to that "hillock in the
sand". When they rose to
charge across the beach, the
Germans opened fire with
at least three large machine
guns. They died in a matter
of minutes. Records are not
clear, but it is thought that
six Bedford boys were among
the twenty-nine, a number
exactly matching the age of
their Captain.*

Defying medical warning, Fellers took them there that day
Infection stricken and weakened, he'd demanded duty's way
He'd sworn to lead the Bedford boys when they first went to the strife
He kept that promise on D-Day and he did it with his life.

*He arose from his infirmary sick bed, the night of 2 June. They were to load up and roll out to the fight in the morning. He had been battling a sinus infection; feverish, weakened and perspiring. A medical officer tried to get him to go to a hospital. He discharged himself and returned to his company. When he appeared in the company mess, they were shocked by his appearance as he shared their pre-departure meal. Here is what he is reported to have said: "I want to go in with the men. If I don't and something happens to those boys, I will never be able to go back to Bedford again"; and then to his assembled company: "I've trained you. I'll die with you too, if it comes to that."*

Now all the beach-bound teams were taking fire, vicious and widespread
More Bedford boys struggled ashore; and most would soon be dead
John Wilkes, their Master Sergeant, fought with bravery to death's call
Taking fire to return it, he raised the standard for them all.

Copyright 2014 - The Bedford Museum and Genealogical Library - Bedford, VA

*John Wilkes was a tough, athletic country boy from a large, struggling, musical and traditional family in which trustworthiness was important. A high school dropout at 16, he worked at feldspar mining and farming, joining the guard when he came of age. His work ethic and discipline, in the style of Taylor Fellers, quickly distinguished him and he was Company A's Master Sergeant before they were activated. Like Fellers, he was a hard-nosed disciplinarian, respected by his men. He made it to the beach and is believed to have died firing his M1 Garand rifle at a German defensive position.*

The last three to land from Bedford; part of Company A's last team
Waded through savage fire to a bloody, chaotic scene
Lieutenant Ray Nance got wounded; his two hometown friends were killed
And he'd mourn their deaths for decades with a sad survivor's guilt.

*Platoon leader and lieutenant Ray Nance was with Company A's headquarters staff; seventeen men in the last of the Company's LCA's to approach the beach, at approximately 6:50 a.m. By then the fire was torrential. Bedford boys John Reynolds and John Clifton were with him. Clifton was hit in the water and disappeared; Reynolds as he stopped in his run across the beach to return fire. Nance was hit in the heel and managed to stagger to shelter under a cliff. He lay there thinking of all his Bedford friends dying or dead within yards of his position. And he thought of them every day for sixty-five years. He died in 2009.*

Nineteen Bedford boys died on D-Day, more than would survive
Five more were soon killed in that fight, just a few were left alive
They came home to share the mourning of a village locked in grief
Still shocked at the greatness of their loss, a price beyond belief.

*Nineteen dead from Bedford on the D-Day beaches, two thousand dead from all of America; close to one of one-hundred from a home to just one in fifty-thousand Americans. Eleven from Bedford lie in the American cemetery at Colleville, overlooking Omaha beach. In 1954, ten years to the day after the battle, Taylor Fellers' mother unveiled a memorial in Bedford of polished granite carved from the Omaha beach cave that had served as the 29th Division's command post. Division Commander General Charles Gerhardt was there and offered these words: "Why was the ll6th picked for that particular job? Because they showed the characteristics necessary to assure success on that particular day. Who were these boys? The record of the 29th Division goes back to 1620, through the regimental history of Virginia troops, and their record has been unequalled. These boys were the descendants of the men who fought with Jackson and Lee and Stuart."*

Four good pairs of brothers, Parker, Stevens, Powers and Hoback
Four families sent eight fighting men, just two of them came back
They stayed close as they prepared for war, in training and on leaves
But brothers to all that searing day for which their town still grieves.

*Roy Stevens and Clyde Powers had been on an LCA that sank before it got to the beach; they were rescued from the water and landed days later. So they survived to embrace their families, not with joy, but in tears for the brothers they had lost.*

The dreadful news flowed into Bedford after a painful wait
Since D-Day, they had prayed and feared for their loved sons' unknown fate
Dread would turn to shock as the news came through, shattering the town
Each Bedford soul knew another in pain, with so many down.

*The weeks after D-Day were filled with anxiety for all and pain for some. The newspapers and radio stations were followed with great intensity. Sporadically, the news came through. The news of Taylor Fellers' death came in a letter from an English friend. Sporadic telegrams arrived, reporting one killed, another missing. On July 15, the Bedford newspaper carried this poem from Fellers' widow:*

*"I mourn for you in silence*
*No eyes can see me weep.*

*But many a silent tear is shed*
*While others are asleep*
*Never did I know that the gift that I sent*
*Would mean so little to you on your birthday, June tenth*
*It will always break my heart and will cause many a tear*
*Just to know your burial day would have been your thirtieth year."*

*Two days later, the dam broke and tragedy flooded Bedford.*

The telegrams came from Roanoke to a drugstore in the square
Western Union's agent was at her desk, in position there
On 17 July, Roanoke warned; casualties were coming
And come they did, relentlessly, the gravity was numbing.

*Elizabeth Teass was just twenty-one years old that Monday in the drugstore. The usual crowd had gathered for morning coffee. The dominating subject was the war and the fate of Company A; they did not know then that only four its original members were still in the fight, none of them Bedford boys. It was 8:30 when Elizabeth switched on her equipment to get the ominous news of impending pain. And then they came, the teletype clatter masking her gasping; nine or ten telegrams.*

While the agent readied those missives in tears and silent shock
She wondered how to get them out before Bedford knew and talked
The drugstore's early patrons became a willing makeshift band
Bringing tragic, silent messages to prayerful, trembling hands.

*Jim Marshall, the sheriff delivered one; so did Pete Rucker, the doctor. Then Elizabeth
called Roy Israel at the taxi company; he delivered several telegrams, always waiting
for company if people were alone; Harold Stevens, older brother of Roy and Ray,
heard the news at his grocery store meat counter and rushed to the drug store to tell
Elizabeth to call him if a telegram came for his mother. It did, within the hour. Roy
was missing in action.*

That was when all of Bedford mourned; the first of many stages
It went on to shape the town in the prisms of the ages
From abject grief to outrage to unmitigated sorrow
To scar-strong hope that future sons would  have a good tomorrow.

*The grieving would take many forms and change over time; it was in fact like an
invisible shroud over a bucolic, beautiful, peaceful and old American village; and the
moving, glinting iridescence would be felt, but not seen.*

Many loved ones would join the mourning; parents, sweethearts, wives
And the only dads, the Parker brothers would not come home alive
So two babies were left to wonder what fathers might have been
In the vacuum of loves lost to war, two journeys would begin.

*Danny Parker, now Heilig, the daughter Earl would never see, dedicated the Company A memorial in 1954 and was present, with Steven Spielberg, at the dedication of the eighty-acre national D-Day memorial in Bedford in 2001. Earl had said he would gladly die if he could just see her. He never did. Peter Parker, now Royce, was two when his father Joseph went to war. Alex Kershaw in his book "The Bedford Boys" puts it well: "In private, of course, Bedford continued to grieve and commemorate. As relatives and widows got older, many tried to rationalize their loss – it was part of a heroic sacrifice that had marked the beginning of the end of Hitler, and America's finest hour. But mostly those left behind still tried to overcome grief that seemed, for some to get greater as their time grew shorter".*

They had died for what they stood for, as Virginians from before
With courage first redeemed at Yorktown, then seen in every war
They'd been with Lee at Gettysburg and MacArthur at the Marne
With the spirit seen on D-Day in the vicious jaws of harm.

But pride much more than grief and pity has marked the Bedford way
And they proudly raise the guidon brought home by Company A
It's a touchstone to remind them when they go to duty's call
Of their long and honored legacy, their reason to stand tall.

*The farmers, clerks and factory hands of Bedford had been volunteers in valiant service to their country for nearly two centuries when their sons landed on Omaha Beach. Their sacrifice that day was poignant and painful, beyond expectation but not commitment. They were ready then as they are today.*

# They Never Came Home...

**Leslie Abbott**

**Wallace Carter**

**John Clifton**

**Frank Draper Jr.**

**Taylor Fellers**

**Charles Fizer**

**Nicholas Gillaspie**

**Bedford Hoback**

**Raymond Hoback**

**Clifton Lee**

**Earl Parker**

**Joseph Parker**

**Jack Powers**

**Weldon Rosazza**

**John Reynolds**

**John Schenk**

**Ray Stevens**

**Gordon White**

**John Wilkes**

**Elmere Wright**

**Grant Yopp**

Additional Bedford men killed on or shortly after D-Day for whom pictures are unavailable: John Dean, Benjamin Hubbard, and Robert Fizer (brother of Charles Fizer). Approximately twelve additional Bedford County men were killed in the European theater.

You can find the spirit of Bedford where trouble riles the world
In America's combat outposts when first her flag's unfurled
From Al Qaeda fights in Kipling's east to skirmishes and wars
Look up!  You may see Bedford's eagle, resplendent as he soars!

*Bedford Museum &*
*Genealogical Library*

They made this poem.  They provided the images of the fallen and more. So
we are grateful to this remarkable memory repository of people and events
which grace the history of southwestern Virginia's county and town named
Bedford. They especially honor the sacrifices of their young men who went
bravely, with a special devotion to duty, into the maelstrom at Omaha
Beach. It was a huge and virtually anonymous gift to the world from a
beautiful and bucolic small American town.

# PREFACE TO POEM
# THE BATTLE OF THE TARAWA ATOLL
# 20 TO 23 NOVEMBER, 1943

The American combat plan which resulted in this battle was first developed in 1930, refined and in place in 1941 when Pearl Harbor was attacked. It essentially called for the Navy and the Marine Corps to start in the Central Pacific, sweep westward and destroy Japanese positions all the way to their homeland. This isn't exactly how it happened.

The Japanese dictated American actions early in the war. American victories were responsive and defensive. The most notable were at Midway and in the Southwest Pacific at Coral Sea and Guadalcanal, all taking place from mid to late 1942. These were the necessary actions that prevented the Japanese from moving beyond the Philippines into Australasia and Australia itself.

In early 1943, implementation of the initial plan began. It had been refined to capitalize on the increasing range and power of our air forces. A major, but not exclusive, focus was placed on islands with airfields. An "island hopping" concept became part of the plan. Our victories could be on islands that could be reached by aircraft from an eastward island.

In early 1943, the 2d Marine Division, bloodied from the battle of Guadalcanal, began arriving in New Zealand to prepare for the Central Pacific offensive.

The Tarawa atoll is a fish-hook shaped cluster of islets with the point of the hook facing west. It is about 50 miles long in each direction, from tip to turn. Betio, at the very tip of the hook is the biggest islet. It is at the Equator, just west of the International Date Line.

Tarawa was not initially in our Central Pacific plan. It was an obscure, copra trading, Micronesian settlement, out of the way and in friendly British hands. That changed in December, 1941 when a Japanese raiding party visited Betio.

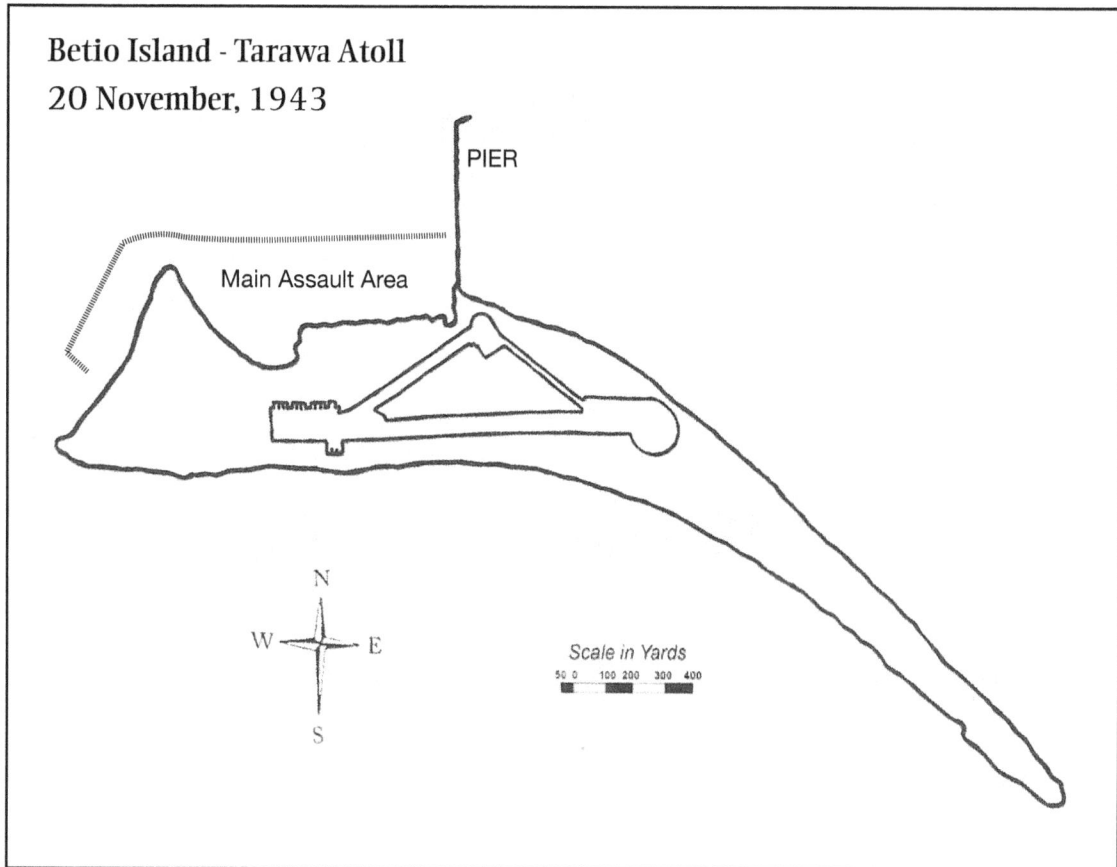

Betio Island - Tarawa Atoll
20 November, 1943

PIER

Main Assault Area

N
W — E
S

Scale in Yards
50 0    100 200   300  400

Shortly after, the few Brits boarded a boat they had hidden and headed to Fiji. Then, a year later, the Japanese arrived in force and began construction of a bomber strip and serious defensive installations.

The Tarawa atoll became a target. Force would be concentrated on Betio. The airstrip would be taken. A conscious decision had been made to give up American lives for quick conquest of an existing airstrip rather than build one in weeks on an empty islet. It would be the first modern amphibious assault against a well defended beachhead. The 2d Division would do the job.

It turned out to be a crucible; a test of these young Americans unlike any they had envisioned. It was the Thanksgiving season at home and they were in hell as we gathered at our hearths.

## TARAWA ATOLL
## 20 TO 23 NOVEMBER, 1943

How many ways do we count the dead? 1,115 Marines, Doctors and Corpsmen. Deconstructing as we must, we lost about 185 per landing zone or battalion; 15 per hour of combat; one every 4 minutes; all in about one square mile of misery. And the enemy lost four times that many. But these are politicians' and journalists' numbers.

Let us count the dead from the beginning in our hearts. Here is the leaden, gray equatorial air in the pre-dawn darkness. Here is an armada of American souls, queued and milling in preparation for a mysterious drama, a tragedy. They have rehearsed but are more uncertain than novice actors in the wings of a foreign theater . . . . .

## 2d MAR. DIV.

Up from New Zealand, troopships in the night
Gun bristling warships, bomb packed carriers
Ten thousand Marines on deck at first light
Abeam of Tarawa's coral barriers.

This Betio sandspit, bunkerpocked wart
Shaped like a rifle, two miles in length
Rigosentai* stuffed, Marine Corps to thwart
The Emperor's legions, boasting of strength.

In stone strong pits under rock covered logs
Groaning abulge with munitions and guns
Grenades and explosives, seething like dogs
Ready, they thought, for America's sons.

*Special Naval Landing Forces or Japanese Marines

"Not a million Marines in 100 years"
Their Admiral Shibasaki had stated
Could win at Tarawa or conquer their fears
Against power that could not be abated.

At sea in the distance our countrymen stood
As flaming shells from their warships were driven
And seeing that fire, they knew as they should
It's a stage set for death and the curtain has risen.

Their awe and their fear turned to focus and action
As they swarmed down the nets to a strange hostile world
Wrenching and pitching, their LC's gained traction
Then lurched to the mission, colors proudly unfurled.

From New York and Texas, Tennessee and Vermont
A cop and a convict, an old China hand
Beacon Hill Brahmins and Okies still gaunt
Miraculous brothers, an impossible band.

Most very young and from everywhere really
Even far distant places, unknown to most
They brought pride and courage, stubborn and steely
A gift we'd soon know and then sadly toast.

At 500 yards out some LC's were halted
Those mean coral reefs rising out of the tide
The miscalculation was bitterly faulted
As sergeants were shouting "go over the side!".

In shoulder high water they dropped and they fell
Then started to wade with their weapons held high
And the fire was on them like bullets from hell
The boat captains watching knew many would die.

Amtracs were sent to go all the way in
Low drafted and treaded they crawled in the surf
Bringing men to the fight again and again
Guns blazing, they growled to their tenuous turf.

Some stayed in the water while others would ride
But all were exposed to death dealing dangers
In those hours of peril, spilling blood in the tide
They were comrades in arms, none of them strangers.

A slender wood pier, stretching out from the shore
Just over the water to just breach the reef
Was quickly co-opted for shelter and more
Marines moving beneath it, finding relief.

Suddenly grappling that pier's ocean end
Two LC's brought a platoon very brave
Scrambling up fast to attack and to send
Its defenders to a watery grave.

This unique and elite Scout and Sniper platoon
Well trained and ready for the combat they'd face
Skilled in the grief they'd be delivering soon
To the enemy's best at a blood measured pace.

William Deane Hawkins was their leader that day
A new First Lieutenant, but brilliant and sure
A beacon of strength as they went to the fray
At age 29, he was wise and mature.

Stubbornly forward, the Leathernecks pressed
On each side of the pier in chaotic bands
In withering fire, America's best
Many died for a stake on Betio's sands.

First Lieutenant Ott Schulte's Amtrac took fire
From a three-sixty arc as beachward it crawled
His two wounded gunners refused to retire
Standing tall to their task, though brutally mauled.

When Lieutenant Jim Fawcett's craft hit the sand
His platoon, though unscathed, had watched others suffer
So they humped on ahead, every last man
Protecting their friends as the battle got rougher.

Some thirty feet wide, their beach-hold was laying
To a seawall of logs, a fortunate shield
Hunkered there knowing the price they were paying
Gut-checking and angry, refusing to yield.

Massive bombardment by sea and by air
Had little effect on those bunkers so strong
Undaunted defenders, in strength, were still there
Seething for combat, both brutal and wrong.

Fallen Marines gently washed by the tide
Others fell in the sand, their backs to the sky
Their comrades fought onward, keeping with pride
The oath for the ages, their bond; "Semper Fi".

Our first waves assaulted the enemy's front
Their first line of bunkers, just over the wall
Crawling over those logs, they went to the hunt
With hand-carried weapons and courage, that's all.

With flamethrowers, rifles, grenades, bayonets
Plans made on the spot in haste and in doubt
Marines viciously calling the enemy's bets
Returning their fire and burning them out.

Sgt. Bill Bordelon, ashore with wave one
Quickly and boldly blew three bunkers away
Though wounded, this Texan, audacious and young
Was charging another when killed the first day.

Major Mike Ryan, in the fight from the start
Led the way out of chaos for many Marines
Brilliant and bold with a warrior's heart
He turned stranded troops into fighting machines.

With a bleeding leg wound and limping ashore
The man in command on the scene in this fight
Colonel David M. Shoup had written the score
Now on stage to conduct, he prayed he'd been right.

Doctors and Corpsmen at heartbreaking work
Unwavering and grim, gentle and stoic
From desperate triage, they never did shirk
The stricken called their commitment heroic.

Milton Meyer was short, a tough PFC
Foot-wounded and lame, "I'll stay here!" he cried
He cursed as he boarded his evac to the sea
It then soon exploded and everyone died.

Flamethrowers were manhandled onto the scene
By hefty Marines who could use them with skill
These fire-spitting, 80 pound grief machines
Brought death in a flash from the hinges of hell.

Young Johnny Borich with one at his back
Faced two wounded foe making uncertain threats
With quick moves, he covered their possible track
Then triggered the fire that cancelled their debts.

Japan's defense was both fluid and static
Strong bunkers with movement by snipers and tanks
Colonel Shoup's team with concern, but not panic
Used real time tactics sent up from the ranks.

Bunker busting Marines would rush to a vent,
Dropping fire and blast  force into its heart
To these nightmarish tasks no one had to be sent,
Unasked volunteers would just pick up and start.

Harry Niehoff, Corporal, TNT trained
Blew big holes in bunkers with his blasting skill
Delivering shock, concussion and pain
Flushing them out where they'd choose to be killed.

Shoup's first action report was carried by hand
At noon on day one with his radios out
"Need men and supplies to take and hold land.
The flow must start now, the issue's in doubt".

General Julian Smith took that request;
A blooded two-star at age 58
He rapidly put his staff to the test;
Before nightfall, relief would be out the gate.

With dusk on day one, the tempo subsided
Marines waited now for a banzai attack
But this night, their concerns were misguided
The battered and shocked Rigosentai held back.

Ignoring the valor they'd faced that day,
With American softness their living lie,
And Imperial hubris their chosen way
They bled for a fiction they'd still not deny.

Just an hour past the second day's dawn
A great fort of supplies had grown on the pier.
Sheltered only by crates, the handlers worked on
Under fire, they brought the food and the gear.

Goods were swarming ashore in one-thousand ways;
Chaotic, ad hoc, ingenious and strained
A great Yankee effort was now on display
Creative fast action, sweat soaked and profane.

Two 900 pound guns appeared on the shore
Needed up front now, beyond the log wall
Two dozen Marines faced fire for the chore
Hoisting'em over, ammunition and all.

Deane Hawkins, twice wounded, led his platoon
As they went to the fight, again and again
This scholar and scrapper had sensed he'd die soon
On day two, he gasped farewell to his men.

1200 Marines, a Major Hays in command
Embarking through hell at sunrise on day two
Were ordered to wade nonstop to dry sand
Leaving casualty care to a follow on crew.

Marines on the beach watched this with dread
While hundreds were hit and dropped out of sight
And the sea turned pink as Americans bled
500, at least, were lost to the fight.

But the combat surged and expanded apace
Rigosentai were now besieged from all sides
And collapsing back from the beaches in haste
As fresh Marine troops surged in through the tides.

Sandy Bonnyman knew the odds were not good
From fortune and Princeton, he was pure volunteer
Leading his troops as a privileged knight would
He died for those men in his 33rd year.

The Japs were confused by constant attacks
Tornadoes of fire, random and wild
This storm front so vicious was breaking their backs
Their composure and pride were being defiled.

And as they moved back, they came into the clear
Firepower found them with lethal effect
While the Navy's big guns arced blast force and fear
Close cannons and mortars shellacked 'em direct.

Pushed to Betio's tip, a small narrow space
Seeking cover in bunkers, foxholes and trees
Their fighting reflecting impending disgrace
Not quitting, but virtually down on their knees.

Their last gasp came the night of day three
A banzai charge which Marines had expected
Rigosentai madly joined the melee,
Knowing they'd finish dead and dejected.

Out came our Marines to fight hand to hand
Bayonets and fists against Japanese swords
With American courage, both tragic and grand
They stood fast and subdued those heathenish hordes.

The last fighting stopped near noon on day four
Setting sons of Japan, broken and solemn
Heard the last crackling notes of this tragedy's score
Broadcast in two tongues, "Betio has fallen".

"Not a million Marines in 100 years"
Shibasaki, you'll recall, had stated
He died with that claim at the scene with his peers
Hubris tattered, in ruins and deflated.

For 76 hours the battle had raged
10,000 horrors in three days of madness
Exhausted Marines commanded the stage
The curtain came down on ruin and sadness.

Congressional Medals of Honor were placed
On four valorous men, each with a story
Though just one survived to tell his with grace
All are etched in the Corps' Legends of Glory.

Bonnyman and Hawkins, Bordelon and Shoup
Blue ribboned stars from this battle so brutal
Now let us tell you of each man in this group
Praying they know that their pain wasn't futile.

In honoring them, we pay homage to all
Who brought Globe and Anchor to Betio's shore
Relentless, they stormed to this crucible's call
Intrepid, they burnished the soul of the Corps.

**Alexander "Sandy" Bonnyman, Jr.** A 33-year old First Lieutenant, son of the President of the Blue Diamond Coal Mining Company in Knoxville, Tennessee. He attended private schools and Princeton where he was a first string football player. This adventure lover was released from the Army Air Corps for buzzing control towers. He owned copper mines in New Mexico, was married with three daughters when he enlisted in the Marines in July, 1942. His medal was awarded to his eldest daughter, Frances, by James M. Forrestal, then Secretary of the Navy, at the Department, in January, 1947.

His citation reads in part: "Determined to effect an opening in the enemy's strongly organized defense line . . . he voluntarily crawled approximately 40 yards forward of our lines and placed demolitions in the entrance of a large Japanese emplacement as the initial move in his planned attack against the heavily garrisoned, bombproof installation . . . Withdrawing only to replenish his ammunition, he led his men on renewed assault, fearlessly exposing himself to the merciless slash of hostile fire as he stormed the formidable bastion .
. . flushing more than 100 of the enemy who were instantly cut down and

effecting the annihilation of approximately 150 troops inside the emplacement . . . assailed by additional Japanese after he had gained his objective, he made a heroic stand on the edge of the structure, defending his strategic position with indomitable determination in the face of the desperate charge and killing three more of the enemy before he fell, mortally wounded."

**William Deane Hawkins.** A 29-year old First Lieutenant raised in Fort Scott, Kansas and El Paso, Texas. Son of a schoolteacher. Brilliant, he won a statewide Chemistry essay contest in high school and was admitted, at 16, to the Texas School of Mines on a full scholarship, graduating with honors. He had been an avowed pacifist until the Japanese attacked. Working as an engineer in Los Angeles, he enlisted three weeks after Pearl Harbor. He had been rejected by other services because of a large burn scar. Recognized quickly as a rising star, he was promoted up from private and selected to lead his Regiment's elite Scout and Sniper platoon.

His citation reads in part: " . . . 1st Lt. Hawkins unhesitatingly moved forward under heavy enemy fire at the end of Betio Pier, neutralizing emplacements in coverage of troops assaulting the main beach positions. Fearlessly leading on to join the forces desperately fighting to gain a beachhead, he repeatedly risked his life throughout the day and night to direct and lead attacks . . . personally initiating an assault on a hostile position fortified by enemy machine guns . . . boldly firing pointblank into the loopholes and completed the destruction with grenades. Refusing to withdraw after being wounded in the chest in this skirmish . . . steadfastly carried the fight to the enemy, destroying three more pillboxes before he was caught in a burst of Japanese shellfire and mortally wounded."

**William James Bordelon.** A 23-year old Staff Sergeant, born on Christmas day, 1920, in San Antonio, Texas, Growing up there, he enlisted three days after Pearl Harbor. A graduate of Central Catholic High School, he had been a cadet officer in the ROTC. He qualified as a Marine Marksman in boot camp, firing a 214 with the old Springfield rifle. His medal was presented to his mother, Carmen, at an impressive ceremony at the Alamo, by President Roosevelt on 17 June, 1944.

His citation reads in part: "Landing in the assault waves under withering enemy fire which killed all but four of the men in his tractor, Sgt. Bordelon quickly made demolition charges and personally put two pillboxes out of action. Hit by enemy fire just as a charge exploded in his hand while assaulting a third position . . . Disregarding his own serious condition, he unhesitatingly went to the aid of one of his demolition men . . . Still refusing aid for himself, he again made up demolition charges and single handedly assaulted a fourth Japanese machine gun position, but was instantly killed when caught in a final burst of fire from the enemy."

**David Monroe Shoup.** A 38-year old Colonel, wrote the Tarawa battle plan and took his Command Post in a trench on Betio as the first waves came ashore, from where he directed all 76 hours of the combat. Born on a farm near Battle Ground, Indiana. Graduated from DePauw University, commissioned a Marine Lieutenant in June, 1926. Served in many roles, at sea and ashore, in the 17 years preceding the battle of Tarawa. Serving in many more roles in the ensuing years, mostly stateside, many at Marine Headquarters, he was promoted up the steps. He was promoted to four star rank and assumed his post as Commandant of the Marine Corps on January 1, 1960. Received his medal from James V. Forrestal, Secretary of the Navy, on 22 January, 1945.

His citation reads in part: "Although severely shocked by an exploding enemy shell soon after landing at the pier and suffering from a serious painful leg wound which had become infected, he fearlessly exposed himself to the terrific and relentless artillery, machine gun and rifle fire from hostile shore emplacements. Rallying his hesitant troops by his own inspiring heroism, he gallantly led them across the fringing reefs to charge the heavily fortified island . . . assumed command of all landed troops and working without rest under constant enemy fire during the next two days, conducted smashing attacks against unbelievably strong and fanatically defended Japanese positions."

> **Back east to Hawaii, troopships in the night**
> **Spaces stand empty, cold, stark and secured**
> **Sleep troubled sailors reflect on the fight**
> **Klaxons blare rudely and then Taps is heard.**

# THE FIRST BATTLE OF BULL RUN

Discord's furious firestorm cleaved a nation's fraying ties
Hope had turned to ashes in the cremation of compromise
Now polarized in enmity, the South chose separation
To keep each state's choice of slavery a righteous expectation.

*"We seek no conquest, no aggrandizement of any kind from the states with which we
were lately confederated. All we ask is to be let alone."*
*Jefferson Davis,*
*April 29, 1861*

The South's brazen moves to disunion exploded in the land
Driving northern will to stop a breach the country could not stand
So with the South's secession and the fear of a war to come
The North made plans like warriors at the sound of beating drums.

*"All wars are planned by old men in council rooms apart; who plan for greater
armament and map the battle chart." Grantland Rice*

A huge tapestry of cotton, of endless rich plantations
A culture, then, of common cause, foundation of a nation
And, yes, the home of a servile class whose labor was enforced
Bringing Christian's crops to market from the seeds that were their source.

*Nine million people were in the South in 1860; 4 million were the slaves who fed the cotton economy. Cotton barons saw looming northern actions as unjustly hostile. Three attempts at compromise had failed. A negotiated solution was not in sight.*

By April, 1861, their secession was complete
Eleven states with bonds being fused in a revolution's heat
This new Confederacy joined with aristocratic pride
Determined that their livelihoods not be threatened from outside.

*In December, 1860, South Carolina became the first. They convinced themselves, these learned, accomplished and religious people, that it was a noble abdication; that they would manage humane elevation of the slaves on their own terms; that it was wrong for others to hypocritically condemn and aggress their social fabric. By late April, it was done. Tennessee was the last to join. The others were Texas, Louisiana, Alabama, Mississippi, Florida, Virginia, Georgia, Arkansas and North Carolina. Missouri, Kentucky and Maryland were called border states. They contributed significant numbers of sympathizers, but did not secede.*

*The Confederate Seal bore the legend "Deo Vindice" meaning, God will vindicate. A sentiment with which northern theologians probably disagreed.*

*In his inaugural address of March 4, 1861, Lincoln said to them:*
*"The Government will not assail you unless you first assail it."*

But the South now saw their slavery at the point of a knife
Which the North would use to pierce, then gut, their southern way of life
To impose unwanted rules on their production and their trade
To break the contracts and traditions from which their lives were made.

*Lincoln's inaugural promise rang hollow in the South. Northern opinion was in flames being fanned by the media. The South knew they would be assailed, militarily, financially and politically.*

They also feared that their rich holdings were lightning rods for fraud
For sacking by lackeys of poseurs, using forged orders from God
They saw northern threats to slavery as a looming Trojan Horse
Seething with blinded rapacity, a dark and dismal force.

*They reckoned that sanctimonious pillaging would come with the slaughter; that evil men would follow the anti-slavery flag bearers.*

The dark clouds of impending war were spreading far and near
And as they gathered, reasoned voices would fade and disappear
To be replaced by metal's clang and the smell of sulphur's fire
And the sight of rushing profiteers with arms makers for hire.

*From South Carolina's secession in December, 1860, through the ensuing months, the talk of war increased with each southern secession. In March, the Confederates put out a call for 100 thousand volunteers. It was quickly oversubscribed with men from every southern state. Arms makers from England and New England were busy soliciting both sides, and munitions inventories were building everywhere.*

ABRAHAM LINCOLN

Intemperate demands were issued in harsh calls to action
Opinion makers fueling fires raging in each faction
The North howled that a war on slavery was ordered by the Lord
And the South growled that their states rights would be guarded by the sword.

*New York Herald, April, 1861...we must send these slave masters, these sinners against human nature our arguments with twelve pounders and mortars."*

*Richmond Enquirer, May 1861: "The sacred soil of Virginia in which repose the ashes of so many of the illustrious patriots who gave independence to their country, has been desecrated by the hostile tread of an armed enemy who proclaims his malignant hatred of Virginia because she will not bow her proud neck to the humiliating yoke of Yankee rule."*

On April 12 at Charleston harbor, cannons were unleashed
Aimed at a small Yankee outpost, but striking the hope for peace
Two hundred men trapped at Fort Sumter, with Union flags unfurled
Were targets of Rebel cannonades, exploding on the world.

*Lincoln had been asked to evacuate Fort Sumter. Instead, on April 8, he announced he was sending medicine and food, but not men and arms. Davis could not brook that move and, four days later, ordered General Pierre Toutant Beauregard, a Louisiana Creole, to bombard that fort. His artillery did, the Yankees surrendered. Three days after the attack, Lincoln called for 75 thousand volunteers, bringing the Union army strength up to match the Confederates'. Blood would soon be spurting forcefully in the winds of war.*

FORT SUMTER

The toxic bile unleashed that day was malignant and it spread
Spawning a seething hunger for war, demanding to be fed
So now, at the north of Virginia, in July's drenching heat
Two armies stood locked and loaded and, sadly, eager to meet.

*Thirty thousand men stood ready on each side. There had been some indecisive earlier
skirmishes. But they all knew that on this day, Sunday, July 21, 1861, they were
meeting in full force.*

They were led by two sons of West Point, of the class of '38
Two generals now at sword point, sharing one ironic fate
They had drilled as brothers on the academy's hallowed grounds
But schemed to ruin each other now for a rage that knew no bounds.

*They were each 43 years old, engaged in a profound irony. Major General
Beauregard's Confederates were to go against Major General Irvin McDowell's
Union army. Beauregard had been 2nd in their class; McDowell 23rd. Neither had
commanded more than 100 men in any situation. They had both been on General
Winfield Scott's staff during the Mexican War.*

And most of their unit commanders were fellow West Point men
Now in a polarized brotherhood, bound for a tragic end
But the honor rolls at West Point join them again today
They led for heartfelt causes, they bled for the Blue and the Gray.

*The Confederates fielded ten brigades of about 3000 men each. Nine of them were commanded by West Point graduates, eight Brigadier Generals and a Colonel.*

*The Union army consisted of four engaged divisions, each of which had two to four brigades of about 3000 men; 13 brigades in total. Thirteen of the seventeen division and brigade commanders were West Point men.*

*The lower ranks, too, were replete with men of West Point.*

*"Hundreds of valiant sons of this beloved alma mater would block it from their consciousness and thus begin the slaughter."*

The Federals marched in pre-dawn darkness down tranquil country roads
With snorting horses yoked to war goods in lethal caisson loads
They'd been told they'd whip the Bull Run Rebels back through Richmond's gate
So Jeff Davis and the world would know that they'd soon seal his fate.

*The Federal troops headed for the battle ground at 2:30 a.m. The Rebels blocked the road at Bull Run Creek. None of them knew the years it would take and the price that would be paid before Jeff Davis would run from Richmond. A few of them were drunk and knew little of anything.*

*And as the sun rose in the sky, scores of civilians from Washington; congressmen and their families, reporters and others, arrived in carriages to witness the battle. They thought the day would be fun; that they were about to witness an easy Union victory. Most of them assembled at a hamlet called Centreville, just east of the expected field of battle.*

They fought in a square of farmland, five miles in each direction
In woods and fields and streams and hills that offered some protection
But death would find its mark that day amidst the lush green bounty
That grew to grace the tables there in old Prince William County.

*The Warrenton Turnpike bisected the battle ground from east to west. Matthews Hill and Henry Hill, where much of the action would take place, were on opposite sides of the pike. A key structure on that road, the Stone Bridge, was almost square in the middle. A road called Manassas-Sudley, bisected north and south. Bull Run Creek meandered through from north to south, mostly in the center. The area was striated with branches of Bull Run Creek and many fords provided easy crossing. The battlefield was about 26 miles southeast of Washington D.C.*

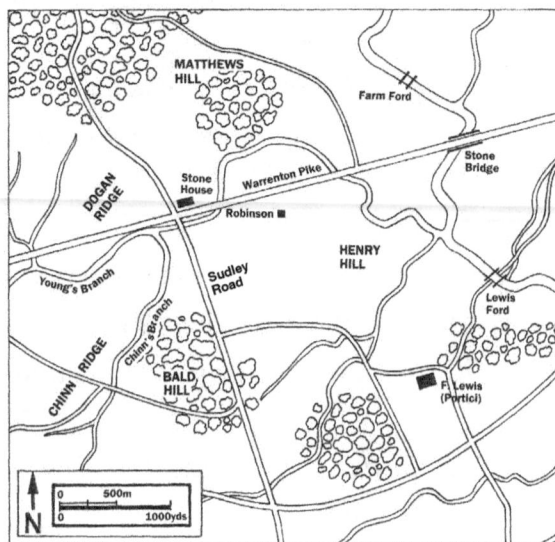

The first three shots were fired from the old Stone Bridge at dawn
The Union's three ton cannon's blasts were heard for miles beyond
Three thirty pound swirling missiles screamed by at the break of day
To shatter a Rebel farmhouse, just half a mile away.

*Those first shots were fired, in fact, by a West Point man: twenty-year old Peter Conover Hains, a fresh graduate of the academy and proud he'd been given command of the massive gun. The Rebel house was an easily defined target and its destruction signaled fearsome Yankee firepower.*

The first moves of the battle were tentative and slow
Union troops followed their cannon's shots and found a hunkered foe
The fight's first probing actions were uncertain and confused
As each struggled to learn the meaning of the other's moves.

*Federal skirmishers followed the cannon's shots across the bridge. They had thought their cannon would force the enemy to flee. That did not happen. But the fight did not escalate. Both commanders had bigger ideas for other places. It was about 6:30 a.m. Both sides were busy gathering intelligence and adjusting their plans. Communication was critical.*

Southern brigades massed in strength, south of the Warrenton Pike
Planning to move northeast, across Bull Run, and make a major strike
They had more strength than the Yankee forces deployed to turn them back
But a communication breakdown would foil the South's attack.

*At 7:00a.m., three Confederate brigades were sent orders to attack across Bull Run and push the Yankees back to Centreville. One brigade never got the word, or never understood it, and the plan failed.*

Union troops, in strength, marched northwest, toward a place called
       Sudley Ford
They used obscure paths as they tried to move unseen and ignored
But a Rebel glimpsed their armor's glint in the sun that morning
And quickly flashed, in semaphore, a short, but urgent warning.

*The message said "Look out for your left. You are turned." An additional 900 rebels were immediately sent to reinforce the two brigades in place. But about 13,000 Union men were on the way. They arrived about 9a.m. and started to cross Sudley Ford. A massive fight at Matthews Hill began an hour later. Two brigades of Rhode Island infantry were in the lead for the Union.*

Decent men, now enemies, some classmates, cousins, brothers
Would now bring the snarl of war, with no mercy, to each other
Here in this place, they'd first see the crimson portent of their fight
For some of them, a final vision as they embraced the night.

*Of course, most of the West Point men and many of the other combatants knew each other. There is no good record of the close relationships that were split by the factions, but there were many. And that, of course, was true throughout the war. When Jeb Stuart, the Confederate Cavalry hero was shaming his own father-in-law, Union General Philip St. George Cooke, at the Chickahominy River, Stuart's comment about General Cooke's anger became legendary: "He will regret it only once and that will be continually."*

At Matthews Hill, the fight's ferocity soon came to full burn
As both sides added guns and men to the combat's vicious churn
But the Federals gained strength faster and took the hard fought hill
The Rebels fell back to fight again. They had not lost their will.

*The Yankee side was making the situation untenable for their enemy. The South's lines were outnumbered and flanked at both ends. The intense Union fire could not be matched. It was now about 11:00a.m. So the order to retreat was given and the Confederates fell back to Henry Hill, about 200 yards south, just east of the Sudley Road.*

They retrenched at a place called Henry Hill, flagging in dismay
The Yankees hollered "victory!", they were sure they'd won the day
But they did not know Stonewall Jackson was on his way with power
His twenty six hundred Virginians were there within the hour.

Jackson's men joined with the veterans of the Matthews Hill fight and formed a defensive line in the trees. Generals Beauregard and Johnston arrived with heavy guns they had commandeered from other units. Jackson directed the activities with his irascible personality. General Barnard Bee is reported to have said "There stands Jackson like a stone wall" and the man then had a new name. General Bee was soon killed in action so the question of whether his remark was a compliment remains unanswered.

Their ranks stretched through timbered hills in the torrid mid-day sun
Young men of the Old Dominion in the land their grand-dads won
They'd lead their comrades back to the fight, and not retreat or pause
With valor born of true belief in the justice of their cause.

*The Confederate line of 3000 men and 13 big guns stretched for half a mile, north to south. The Union troops were dispersed in an area about half a mile to the northwest. The Virginians and their friends were in good tree cover and they were ready to fight.*

The Yankees probed that Rebel line to provoke a firefight
And in a fierce southern salvo, the Federals saw the light
The South was shooting from tree cover at Yanks in open ground
And in just twenty vicious minutes, the North was turned around.

*At 1:00pm the federal command sent two regiments, about 1000 men, across Sudley Road to test the southern end of Jackson's tree line. The Rebels opened with a volley; the Yanks returned fire, but lost men and could not find cover. It was over in twenty minutes.*

The Yanks then brought artillery across the Sudley Road
And deafening rounds from a big gun fight started to explode
The North rolled their cannons in to about 400 yards
Their first rounds killed old Judith Henry and blew her home to shards.

*There were eleven Federal guns of varying power in two separate units. It was about 2:00pm. Confederate sharpshooters in Mrs. Henry's doomed house were targeting the North's gun crews. The Union poured regiments in and a series of infantry attacks and counter attacks, charges and retreats ensued. The Rebels wanted to take the Union guns. The battlefield turned into a holocaust.*

The two sides joined and slithered like a rattlesnake's convulsions
Serpentine and hand to hand, advancement and repulsion
Warriors watched their blood commingle in viscid, turgid bursts
In undulating ghastly visions of combat at its worst.

*They fought all over Henry Hill, but at different times with different units. Units would retreat and others of their ranks would advance in other places. "Give them the bayonet!" would ring out before the brief, determined, hand to hand encounters. Both sides were disorganized, but the Confederates had the advantage of tree cover. They had arrived at Henry Hill first and owned the battlefield. The Yankees had to take it.*

The cacophony of combat enveloped the grassy field
The sides stood strong against each other, but one began to yield
The air was filled with rifle reports and vulgar cannon blasts
And the anguished cries of men and horses falling in the grass.

*All the combat was furious. General Beauregard's horse was shot out from under him and two of his top commanders were killed. Yankee Colonel James Cameron, brother of the Secretary of War Simon Cameron, was killed. Stonewall Jackson was wounded. One of the Union's artillery battery commanders was wounded, And the men of the ranks were falling while their brothers kept fighting. The Federals had no place to hide, except in retreat back over Sudley Road. They were crossing it in both directions, but the backward flow grew greater.*

Capture of the Yankee guns was a key Rebel goal that day
They wanted to shoot'em at their owners as they ran away
Those guns changed hands four brutal times that bloody  afternoon
But in the end, the Rebels had'em; the fight would finish soon.

*The Yankees lost their last fight for the guns at about 4:00 p.m. The Rebels did, in fact, turn one of the guns around and fire at an enemy position. The first Union brigades started to withdraw up the Sudley road. Others came back to join the fight from across the road and the Confederates, now even stronger with reinforcements, came off of Henry Hill to attack.*

The uncertainty was lifting  on the downside of this day
The combat scales were tipping now to the stubborn men in gray
The Richmond road ran on south, but the fight would soon turn northward
And the specter of a horrid war started to come forward.

*Now, at about 4:30, both sides knew the die was cast and the Union's rank and file were increasingly difficult to motivate.*

As the Federals fled the onslaught, seeking some protection
Their will to turn and attack again crumbled in dejection
Their mood turned dark, like clotting blood, on this day so brutal
And then they knew that fighting on would be both bleak and futile.

*The last Union regiments in place west of the Sudley road, made an honorable stand against a new Confederate attack. Facing fire at 200 yards with hope gone, the last stand of Federal men finally took it upon themselves to go north toward safety.*

In chaotic gangs, they started north, their leaders lost command
To the Warrenton Pike they went, a scattered, frightened band
They headed east past Matthews Hill and the bridge that spanned Cub Run
Escaping back to Washington, where their Government was stunned.

*Panic stricken soldiers began to throw away their weapons as they headed east. They joined hundreds of civilian spectators fleeing eastward. Wagons and artillery were abandoned, including the three-ton gun that had fired the opening shots twelve hours earlier.*

*General McDowell stopped to pen a message to one of his staff officers. He conceded that their army was a confused, hungry mob, low on ammunition. He suggested they would make a last stand at Fairfax Court House. They never did.*

*That night, Lincoln and his cabinet got a telegram: "McDowell and his army in full retreat through Centreville. The day is lost."*

*Jefferson Davis telegraphed Richmond "We have won a glorious, but dear-bought victory. Night closed in on the enemy in full retreat and closely pursued."*

*494 Union troops had been killed in action; 418 Confederates. The smell of blood was in the wind. The next day, 22 July, Lincoln's congress asked for 500 thousand volunteers; Jeff Davis's asked for 400,000.*

The Union cowered in defeat, the Confederates took heart
From this first test of the strength required for them to stay apart
But soon both sides would face the fact that chance can affect a fight
And their bets would cost them dearly 'til the end came in to sight.

*The future careers of the leading generals at Bull Run were modestly successful or less than that. McDowell was blamed by many for the Union loss. He was relegated to support roles. Beauregard was slighted by Jefferson Davis, probably because of impolitic utterances. He received only one more top command and was finally in a figurehead role. But he was ordered, in 1864, to defend Petersburg, Virginia from capture from Grant, which he did successfully.*

*Most of the commanders from West Point would go on to many of the historic and bloody battles now in their vision. They are, of course, in the academy's long gray line and a palpable presence there, even now.*

*Erasmus Keyes, who would battle for the Union at Gettysburg.*

Erasmus Keyes

*David R. Jones, who would fight for the South at the Seven Days Battles, Second Bull Run and Antietam.*

David R. Jones

*James Longstreet, who would battle for the South at Second Bull Run, Antietam, Fredericksburg, Gettysburg, Chickamauga, Knoxville and more.*

James Longstreet

William Tecumseh Sherman

*William Tecumseh Sherman, who would be in nine more campaigns on the Union side, including Shiloh, Vicksburg, Chattanooga and the march from Atlanta to the sea.*

Israel Richardson

*Israel B. Richardson, who would fight for the Union at Second Bull Run, various skirmishes in Northern Virginia and then at Antietam where he was mortally wounded.*

Jubal Early

*Jubal Early, Confederate warrior. He fought in the Seven Days battles, Second Bull Run, Antietam, Fredericksburg and Gettysburg.*

Nathan "Shanks" Evans

*Nathan George Evans, another Confederate He liked whiskey and was often followed by an aide with a jug of it. He fought at Second Bull Run, South Mountain and Antietam; and then on to campaigns in Eastern North Carolina.*

Orlando Wilcox

*Orlando Wilcox, Union, earned the Medal of Honor at Matthews Hill; was wounded and captured. released a year later. He went on to fight at Antietam, Knoxville and Petersburg.*

*Jeb Stuart, Confederate cavalry commander. He rode on with his colorful cavalier cape and cocked hat through the Peninsula and Northern Virginia campaigns, Antietam, Fredericksburg, Chancellorsville and Gettysburg; finally to be mortally wounded at the battle of Yellow Tavern.*

Jeb Stuart

*Thomas "Stonewall" Jackson. Went on to fight for the South in many more places including the Valley Campaign, the Seven Days Battles, Rappahannock Station and Second Bull Run. He was mortally wounded by his own sentries at the Battle of Chancellorsville.*

Thomas "Stonewall" Jackson

They all then knew they'd had a glimpse of the vicious times ahead
They'd lost their natures' better angels, finding demons instead
The weeks and months would turn to years of unmitigated dread
Six hundred twenty five thousand souls, the army of the dead.

Those deaths would pummel the Southland and besiege the Northland too
And in union now, we sing of them; the good men and the true.

## ABOUT THE AUTHOR

Tom Pettit was raised in Kansas and attended Kansas University. He was managing editor of their 1958 yearbook, "The Jayhawker".

He is the son of a journalist and an advertising creative director. He is the grandson of Minnie Grinstead, first woman in the Kansas legislature, WCTU lecturer, Baptist minister, pioneer suffragist and ardent prohibitionist. He occasionally raises a glass in her honor. He is a member of Mensa.

After graduating first in his class from the Navy's Hospital Corps School, he served two years of active duty.

He spent a 40 year career as a marketing and advertising executive and consultant. His first job was with Procter & Gamble. Other major consumer product companies have used his talents, including Dole, Mattel, Nestle, American Home Products, St. Ives Laboratories, Colgate, Clorox and more. He has written dozens of marketing plans, reams of advertising and promotional copy, and many sales presentations. He has also written essays and poetry for a private club's literary periodical.

Four of his inventions are used in consumer product promotion programs, including the patented Surprise Value Refund Form.

In 2012, he published a 5-star book for kids: "26 POEM-STORIES ABOUT ANIMALS, A to Z, Aardvark to Zebra". The website is www.tompettitpoems.com

Tom and his wife Lynn have lived in the same house in Palm Springs, CA, for 38 years. They have two adult daughters and two cats.

## SOURCES FOR "HARM'S WAY TRILOGY" — AUTHOR'S NOTES

The poems are informed by a host of memories from books, articles and conversations that took place over 70 years. It all started in 1944, when mom came home from having just seen the shocking, and later legendary, "Technicolor" newsreel about Tarawa. I was 10 years old. And our conversation that day became a deep deposit in my memory bank.

The books I used in close preparation are:

Hammel and Lane, *Bloody Tarawa*, Pacifica Press

Kershaw, *The Bedford Boys: One American Town's Ultimate D-Day Sacrifice*, Da Capo Press

Morrison, *Bedford Goes to War*, Warwick House

Davis, *Battle at Bull Run: A History of the First Major Campaign of the Civil War*, L.S.U. Press

www.ingramcontent.com/pod-product-compliance
Lightning Source LLC
Chambersburg PA
CBHW080946050426
42337CB00056B/4846